THE WEATHER SKY

PHOTOGRAPHED, ILLUSTRATED, AND WRITTEN BY

Bruce McMillan

A Sunburst Book • Farrar Straus Giroux

For Brett

This book was photographed in Maine. The weather patterns, types of clouds photographed, and weather facts apply to all of Earth's temperate climates.

The weather facts and cloud identifications were verified by Thomas Emerson, Fred Ronco, and Charles H. Smith of the National Weather Service Forecast Offices in Boston, Massachusetts, and Portland, Maine, and Dr. John T. Snow, of the Department of Earth and Atmospheric Sciences, Purdue University.

All photos were taken in Shapleigh, Maine, an area the Portland office of the National Weather Service refers to as "thunderstorm alley." A Nikon F camera with a 24, 28, 35, 50, or 105mm Nikkor lens and a polarizing filter, if needed, was used. The film was Kodachrome 25, processed by Kodalux.

The cloud illustrations were airbrushed using a Paasche VL airbrush on Bristol Board with black Sumi ink and highlighted with white opaque.

The selection of the sequence of the seasons is in honor of my childhood memory of Princess Summerfall Winterspring.

Published in Canada by HarperCollins*CanadaLtd*
Color separations by Imago Publishing Ltd.
Printed and bound in the United States of America
Designed by Bruce McMillan
First edition, 1991
Sunburst edition, 1996

Library of Congress Cataloging-in-Publication Data
McMillan, Bruce.
The weather sky / photographed, illustrated, and written by Bruce McMillan.
— 1st ed.
p. cm.
Summary: A study of weather patterns and clouds that occur in the Earth's temperate zones.
1. Weather—Juvenile literature. 2. Clouds—Identification—Juvenile literature. [1. Weather. 2. Clouds.] I. Title.
QC981.3.M45 1991 551.6—dc20 90-56151 CIP AC

WEATHER

Weather is the state of the atmosphere on our planet at a specific place and time. It's sun and warmth. It's clouds and rain. It's cold and snow.

Many of our decisions are based on what the weather will be in the near future. Will rain postpone the baseball game? Will an ice storm close the airport? Will a snowstorm cancel school?

Weather forecasts are made by meteorologists. They gather information about the earth's atmosphere from weather instruments and satellites. Using this information, records of past weather patterns, and their understanding of nature, meteorologists predict the weather. With today's improved technology and computers, weather forecasts are more accurate than they used to be. Yet they aren't always 100 percent accurate because what is seen in the sky, and the weather associated with it, is influenced by many things. Among these are air currents, the earth's rotation, local conditions, seasons, the surface of the earth, and time of day. With so many things interacting to produce our weather, it's not possible to predict the weather with complete accuracy.

A major influence on our weather, and often on the clouds we see that are associated with a change in it, is that of weather fronts. This book shows the effects of the simplest weather fronts and the clouds associated with these fronts. It explains what is seen in the sky and how this relates to the common weather map.

WEATHER MAPS

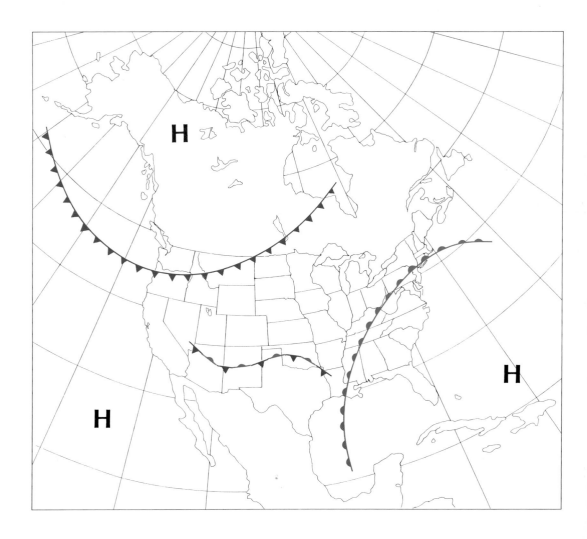

Weather maps often appear in newspapers and on television. They are used throughout the world. They are based on information gathered by meteorologists. Using letters and symbols, weather maps show the present weather conditions and provide clues to future changes in the weather. What do the letters and symbols represent?

The lowest layer of the earth's atmosphere is the weather zone. It's made up of air masses, and it extends from the ground up to about ten miles in the sky. Our planet's gravity holds the weather zone in place.

Air masses are large bodies of air. They cover our entire planet like giant soap bubbles hundreds of miles in diameter. An air mass has layers of about the same temperature and the same moisture throughout. The temperature and moisture are affected by where the air mass forms over the earth's surface. For example, a desert is usually hot and dry, so a warm, dry air mass can develop over it. A tropical ocean is warm and wet, so a warm, wet air mass can develop over it. An arctic ocean is cold and wet, so a cold, wet air mass can develop over it.

Air masses are constantly moving across the earth's surface, changing temperature and shape. This movement is influenced primarily by two things—the sun and the rotation of the earth. The sun heats our planet's surface more at the equator than at the North and South Poles. Because warmed air rises and cooled air sinks, at the equator the air rises and flows north and south toward the poles. At the polar regions, cooled air sinks and moves toward the equator. While this north–south air movement is taking place, there is also eastward movement of the ground—our planet is rotating. It is this combination—north–south air movement and eastward planetary rotation—that causes the air masses to move.

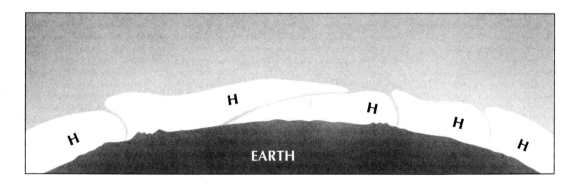

HIGHS

Air masses are dome-shaped and made up of air molecules. There are more air molecules at the center of the dome than at the edges. More air molecules mean more weight—more air pressure. So the high-pressure, central area of an air mass is appropriately called a high. On the weather map, the high is shown with an "H." A high often means clear skies and sunny weather, but—as with so many things about the weather—not always.

FRONTS

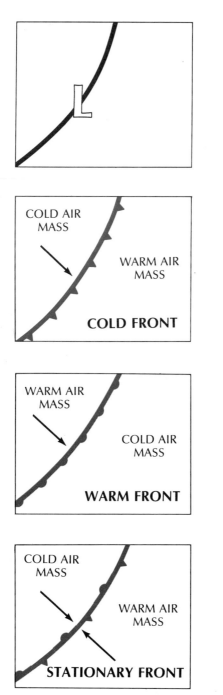

A front is where the edges of two air masses of different temperatures meet. It's like the surface formed when two soap bubbles touch and push against each other, but don't pop. Most weather changes take place as a front passes by.

The air molecules at the edge of an air mass are not packed as closely together as they are at the central area of an air mass. Because of this, the air pressure is lower where two air masses meet. Frontal lows are the active "weather makers." The mutual boundary of low pressure, the front, is shown as a line on the weather map. Sometimes, along the front there are places where the air pressure is very low. These frontal lows are shown on the weather map with the letter "L." Many times, there isn't an area of significant low air pressure along a front, so there isn't an "L" marked on the weather map.

A cold front and a warm front are the simplest kinds of fronts. They can occur at any time of the year. For example, the term "cold front" refers to the relatively cooler temperatures of the approaching air mass for that season. In the summer, it might bring a cooler summer day. In the winter, it might bring a frigid winter day. Besides a temperature change, if a front is approaching—whether it's a cold front or a warm front—it usually means the weather will be changing. A storm could be coming.

If the advancing air mass is a cold air mass, the leading edge, the cold front, is shown on the weather map as a blue line with small triangles. The blue triangles point in the direction that the cold air mass is moving.

If the advancing air mass is a warm air mass, the front is shown as a red line with small half circles. The red half circles, like the cold-front triangles, show the direction in which the air mass is moving.

If a front is stalled, meaning that neither the warm nor the cold air mass on opposite sides of the front is advancing, it's called a stationary front. On the weather map, the blue triangles point away from the cold air mass, and the red half circles point away from the warm air mass. A stationary front usually means that the weather, whatever it is, will remain the same.

Warm air is lighter than cold air. How does this affect the front?

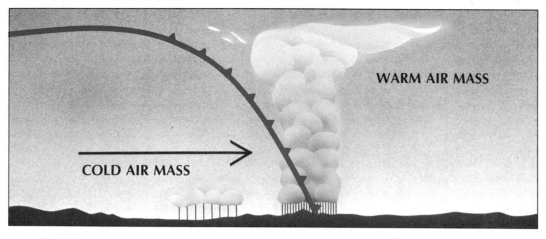

Cold fronts have greater temperature and pressure differences between the two air masses than warm fronts. This greater difference causes the high behind the cold front to push the front forward faster. The bubble of heavier cold air pushes under the lighter warm air. It lifts the warm air upward, and there is less dragging of the air masses along the ground to slow the forward movement. Because cold fronts move quickly across the earth's surface, weather changes usually occur faster, and storms will soon pass by.

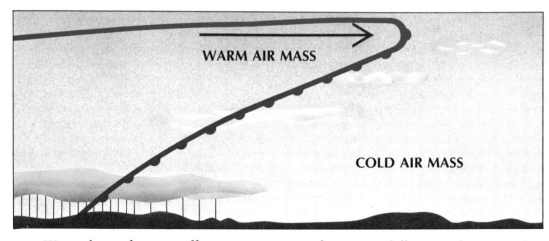

Warm fronts have smaller temperature and pressure differences between the two air masses. There is less of a pushing force from the high behind the warm front. When a warm front advances toward a cold air mass, the leading edge of the bubble of warm air rises over the cold air. It stretches out like a wedge as the warm air keeps pushing forward, over the cold air, and the cold air mass drags along the earth's surface. This dragging slows the movement of the front even more. With slow-moving warm fronts, weather changes usually take longer to occur, and it may rain or snow for a longer time.

CLOUDS

What does it feel like inside a cloud? When you take a walk on a foggy day, you are walking through a ground-level cloud called fog. It feels damp because a fine mist of moisture droplets surrounds you. You can pass right through it, just as a plane passes through a cloud in the sky.

A cloud is a visible mist of billions of water droplets or ice particles floating in the sky. These water droplets or ice crystals are smaller and much lighter than fine sand. A cloud forms when there's enough moisture in the air and the conditions are right for the moisture to condense into water droplets or ice crystals. Because each droplet of moisture is so small and weighs so little, it doesn't fall. It floats in the weather zone. When billions of these floating, miniature moisture droplets are seen grouped together, they appear as a cloud.

Everywhere, except at the warm equator, rain and snow start as ice crystals in a cloud. In a winter cloud, the ice crystals fall through the cloud and grow. They become snowflakes. In a summer cloud, the ice crystals melt as they fall into the lower, warmer air. They combine with other droplets and become rain.

Clouds often occur along weather fronts. When this happens, usually certain types of clouds appear in a predictable order. When a cold front approaches, clouds develop low in the sky and billow upward. When a warm front approaches, clouds form high in the sky, and as the warm front continues to pass by, other types of clouds form lower and lower in the sky.

All clouds are found slightly lower in the sky during the winter and slightly higher in the sky during the summer. That's because the height of the weather zone changes with the temperature. Cold winter air is heavier. So in winter the weather zone compresses and sinks closer to the ground. But in summer the air is warmer, so the top of the weather zone stays higher.

THE CLOUDS IN THE WEATHER SKY

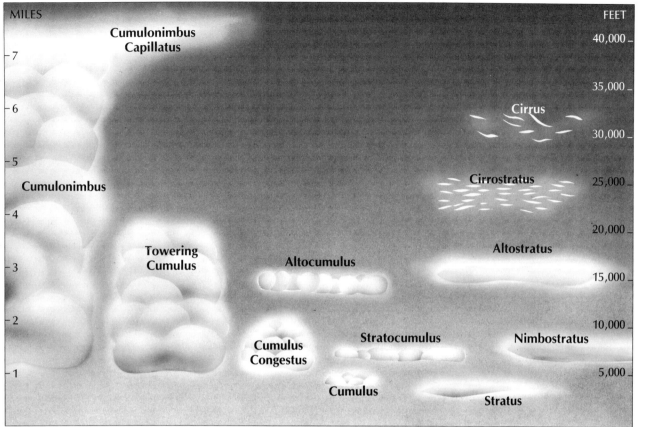

MILES
- 7
- 6
- 5
- 4
- 3
- 2
- 1

Cumulonimbus Capillatus

Cumulonimbus

Towering Cumulus

Altocumulus

Cumulus Congestus

Cumulus

Stratocumulus

Stratus

Cirrus

Cirrostratus

Altostratus

Nimbostratus

FEET
40,000
35,000
30,000
25,000
20,000
15,000
10,000
5,000

CLOUD HEIGHT

HIGH

MIDDLE

LOW

High-altitude clouds: cirrus and cirrostratus clouds.
Middle-altitude clouds: altocumulus and altostratus clouds.
Low-altitude clouds: nimbostratus, stratus, stratocumulus,
and cumulus clouds (including cumulus congestus).

Exceptions to this cloud classification by height are the most dramatic clouds. They are towering cumulus and cumulonimbus rain clouds. Cumulonimbus clouds are often thunderstorm clouds. They can be ten or more miles in height, extending vertically through all heights: low, middle, and high.

WATCHING THE WEATHER SKY

These descriptive words and parts of words from the name of a cloud tell more about that cloud. For example, an altostratus cloud is a middle-height cloud (alto-), and it's a flat, layered cloud (-stratus). The names are based on Latin words.

alto-	It's a middle-height cloud. *Altus* in Latin means "height."
capillatus	It's the top, or cap, of the cumulonimbus cloud. *Capillatus* in Latin means "hairy"—and its leading edge often looks like wispy strands of hair.
cirro- or -cirrus	It's a high, wispy cloud made up of ice crystals. *Cirrus* in Latin means "curl," and cirrus clouds often streak across the sky in swirling curls.
congestus	It's likely forming into a towering cumulus or cumulonimbus cloud. *Congestus* in Latin means "heaped together," and that's how the cloud looks—congested.
cumulo- or -cumulus	It's a puffy cloud that looks like floating cotton balls. *Cumulus* in Latin means "heap," and, indeed, these clouds look like heaps of cotton balls.
nimbo- or -nimbus	It's a dark rain or snow cloud. *Nimbus* in Latin means "rainstorm."
strato- or -stratus	It's a flat, layered cloud. *Stratus* in Latin means "spread out."

It's a humid summer day. You can feel the dampness in the air. This means you are in a hot, wet air mass. The pale blue sky shows that the air is full of moisture in the form of water vapor. But no clouds are present. According to the weather map for your area, this could change soon. The place from where you are viewing the sky, as seen in the photograph, is marked on the weather map by a dot at the center. On the weather map you can see that far away from your viewing place a cold front is approaching. A change in the weather is about to take place. A fast-moving storm is on the way.

Local-Area
Weather Map

SKY VIEWING
PLACE
•

HOT, MOIST
AIR MASS

/11

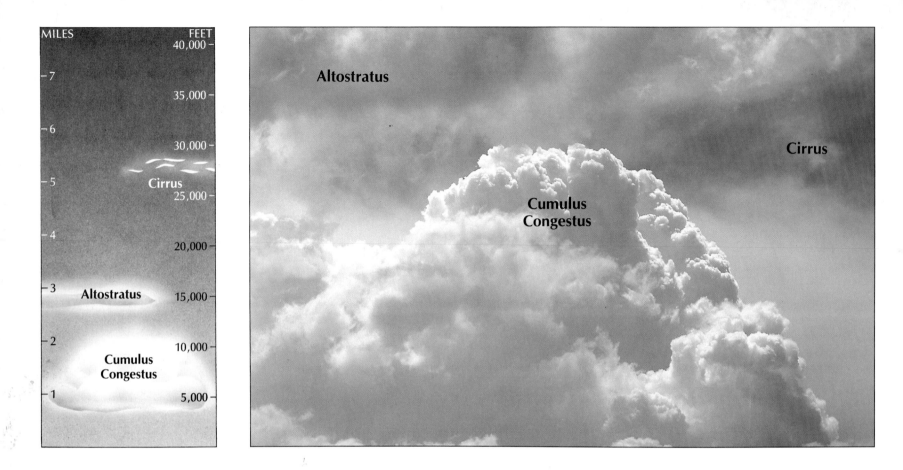

MILES | FEET
7 — | 40,000 —
 | 35,000 —
6 — | 30,000 —
 | Cirrus
5 — | 25,000 —
4 — | 20,000 —
3 — Altostratus | 15,000 —
2 — | 10,000 —
Cumulus Congestus |
1 — | 5,000 —

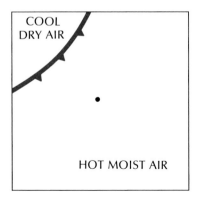

COOL DRY AIR

•

HOT MOIST AIR

Clouds associated with fronts usually occur in a predictable sequence. With a cold front, the clouds begin lower in the sky and expand upward. As this cold front gets closer to your viewing place, the cool air mass pushes under the warm, wet air mass, causing cumulus congestus clouds to form. These clouds are full of moisture. They are typical of summertime cold fronts advancing on warm, moist air. Though other cloud types sometimes appear at the same time in the sky, one type usually predominates. Here it is the cumulus congestus clouds.

Cumulonimbus

As the front keeps approaching, the cumulus congestus clouds expand and billow miles upward. They become cooler and turn into tall cumulonimbus rain clouds. The expanding air inside the clouds means the molecules of the clouds are moving farther away from one another. This expansion causes the clouds to cool. As the clouds cool, the moisture inside them condenses into ice crystals and water droplets. Some of these droplets grow larger and combine with one another. The clouds become darker. When the droplets become heavy enough, too heavy to float in the air anymore, they fall as raindrops.

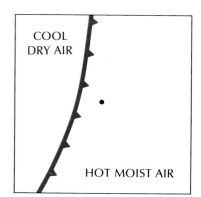

COOL
DRY AIR

HOT MOIST AIR

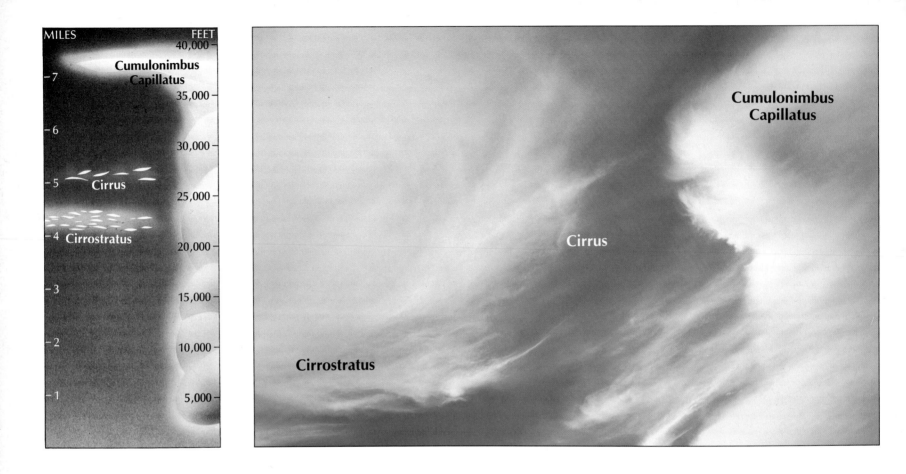

MILES | FEET

40,000

Cumulonimbus Capillatus

— 7

35,000

— 6

30,000

— 5 **Cirrus**

25,000

— 4 **Cirrostratus**

20,000

— 3

15,000

— 2

10,000

— 1

5,000

Cumulonimbus Capillatus

Cirrus

Cirrostratus

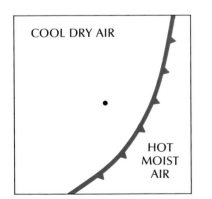

COOL DRY AIR

HOT MOIST AIR

At ground level, it's a warm summer day and it's raining. But high in the sky, at the top of the cumulonimbus rain clouds, it's quite cold. Instead of water droplets at the top of these clouds, there are ice crystals. The top, or cap, of the cloud is called capillatus. Seen from the side, it often looks something like an anvil. Its ice crystals get blown ahead of the rest of the cloud beneath it, forming the point of the anvil. The leading edge of the cap—the anvil's point—often appears as wispy streaks. They blow in the direction of the upper-level winds. This isn't necessarily the same direction that the front is moving in.

Cumulus

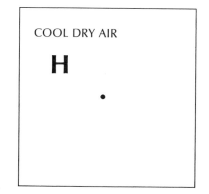

MILES   FEET
40,000 –
– 7
35,000 –
– 6
30,000 –
– 5
25,000 –
– 4
20,000 –
– 3
15,000 –
– 2
10,000 –
– 1   5,000 –
Cumulus

The central area of the cold air mass, the high, has arrived. It has pushed the cold front away and brought fair weather. Though there is no front present, local conditions have caused low-altitude cumulus clouds to form. This is typical for a sunny summer afternoon. The sun shines on the earth's surface, warming it. By afternoon, the now-warm ground heats the air above it. The warmed air rises, and cools. With this cooling, the moisture in the air condenses as tiny droplets of water, making cumulus clouds. Because there's barely enough moisture present for them to form, they won't become rain clouds. During the afternoon, they develop and evaporate back into the atmosphere, repeatedly, usually disappearing entirely by evening, when the sun goes down and the earth's surface cools.

COOL DRY AIR

H

•

/15

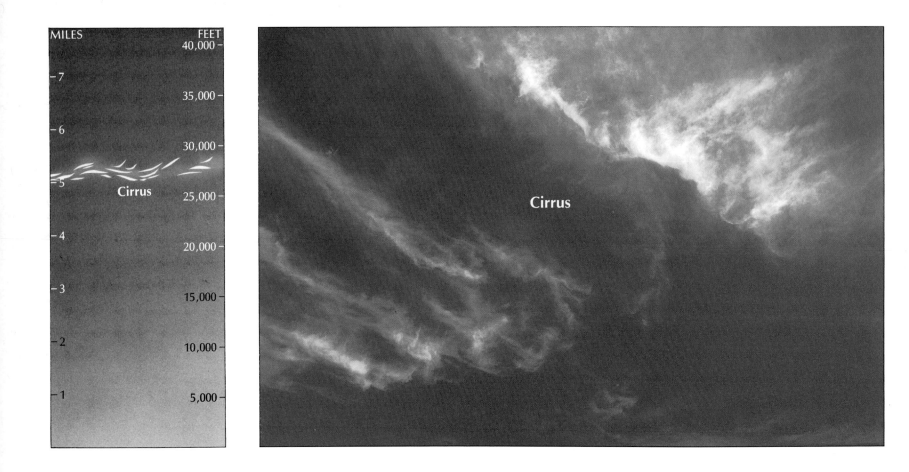

MILES   FEET
40,000 –

– 7

– 6   35,000 –

30,000 –

– 5   **Cirrus**

25,000 –

– 4

20,000 –

– 3   15,000 –

– 2   10,000 –

– 1   5,000 –

Cirrus

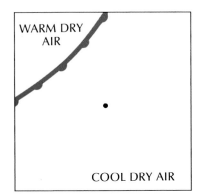

WARM DRY
AIR

COOL DRY AIR

It's a different summer day. You can see on the weather map that a warm front is approaching. High in the sky there are cirrus clouds. A few cirrus clouds sometimes form when a weak warm front arrives, and there is usually no dramatic change in the weather. Fronts can be weak or strong. If the change in temperature across a front is gradual, the front is weak. A weak front is often barely noticeable. If the temperature change is abrupt, the front is strong. A strong front usually brings a dramatic change in the weather. Warm fronts are weaker than cold fronts.

Cumulus

Cumulus

MILES

FEET

40,000 —

—7

35,000 —

—6

30,000 —

—5

25,000 —

—4

20,000 —

—3

15,000 —

—2

10,000 —

—1

5,000 —

Fall is here. The temperatures of the warm and cold air masses are seasonably cooler than they were in the summer. A cold front is approaching, producing low-altitude cumulus clouds. Inside the clouds, air currents billow upward, producing rounded mounds at the top. But the bottoms of the clouds are flat. They are flat because the temperature layer below the clouds is too warm for moisture to condense into water droplets.

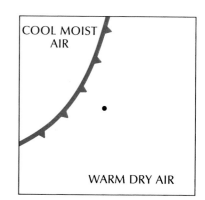

COOL MOIST
AIR

WARM DRY AIR

MILES   FEET
40,000 –

– 7

35,000 –

– 6

30,000 –

– 5

25,000 –

– 4

20,000 –

– 3

15,000 –

Towering Cumulus

– 2

10,000 –

– 1

5,000 –

Towering Cumulus

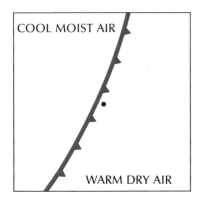

COOL MOIST AIR

WARM DRY AIR

It's raining. The cold front has arrived, causing the towering cumulus clouds of a storm. If there were more moisture in the air, and if the front had been stronger, the towering cumulus clouds might have continued to billow upward and become cumulonimbus rain clouds.

Stratocumulus

MILES | FEET
40,000 –
– 7
35,000 –
– 6
30,000 –
– 5
25,000 –
– 4
20,000 –
– 3
15,000 –
– 2
10,000 –
– 1   Stratocumulus   5,000 –

The cold front has passed by. It's no longer raining. The cool air mass pushes across the earth's surface. Puffy layers of stratocumulus clouds formed from the remains of the rainstorm's moisture are all that is left of the rainstorm. No matter what time of year, it always feels cooler after a cold-front rainstorm. Cold air is brought down to ground level from the mid-level of the weather zone by the falling raindrops. Then the arrival of the cool air mass brings cool weather over the next twelve to forty-eight hours.

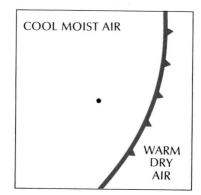

COOL MOIST AIR

WARM DRY AIR

MILES
FEET
40,000 —
— 7
35,000 —
— 6
30,000 —
— 5
25,000 —
— 4
20,000 —
— 3
15,000 —
— 2
10,000 —
— 1
5,000 —
Stratocumulus

Stratocumulus

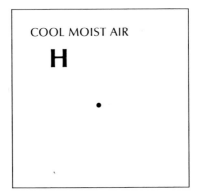

COOL MOIST AIR

H

The center of the cool air mass, the high, is approaching. This high and the decreasing number of stratocumulus clouds indicate that fair weather is probably on the way.

COOL DRY AIR

H

·

This fall sky has very little moisture in it. The deep blue color shows that a dry air mass is present. White sunlight is made up of the colors red, orange, yellow, green, blue, indigo, and violet. Skies look deep blue because the blue part of the sun's light bounces off the air molecules when it enters the atmosphere. All the other colors pass through. If water vapor was present, these other colors would bounce off the water vapor molecules, making the sky appear a lighter, whitish blue, as it did in the sky of a humid summer day.

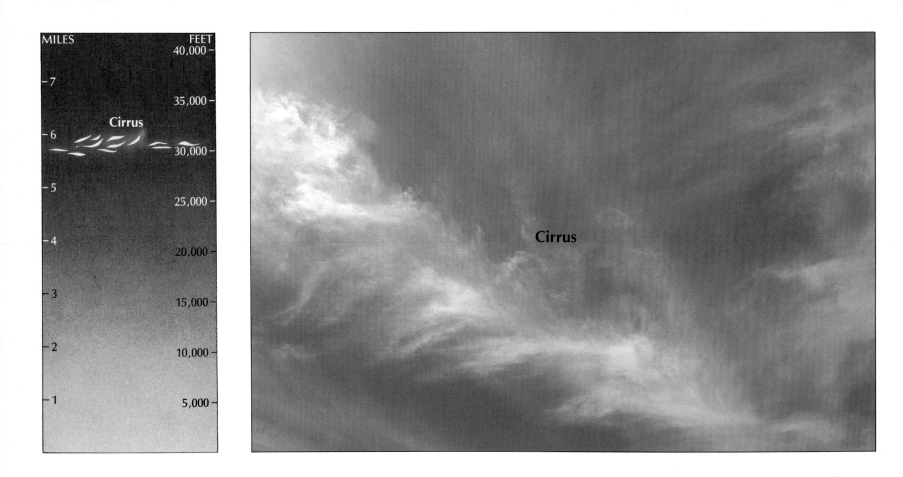

MILES | FEET

40,000 —

— 7

35,000 —

Cirrus

— 6
30,000 —

— 5
25,000 —

— 4
20,000 —

— 3
15,000 —

— 2
10,000 —

— 1
5,000 —

Cirrus

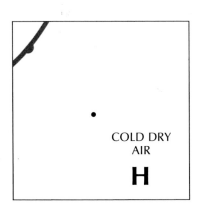

COLD DRY
AIR

H

It is winter. A warm air mass is advancing against a cold air mass. As the warm air mass rises over the cold air mass, the leading edge at the top of the warm-air-mass wedge arrives at your viewing place first. It's high in the sky. A predictable sequence of clouds will occur, starting high in the sky and dropping lower toward the ground, as the warm air mass advances. Here, the high cirrus clouds, the first clouds to appear in a warm-front sequence, are an indication that a warm front is approaching.

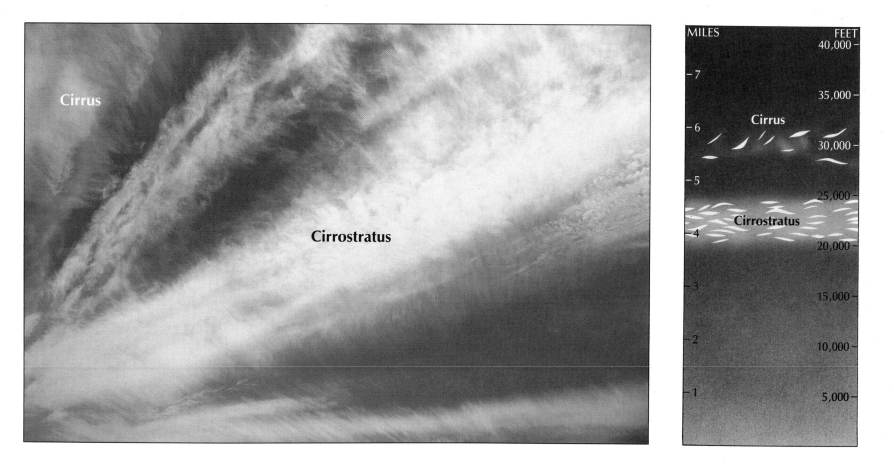

Cirrus

Cirrostratus

MILES   FEET
40,000 –
–7
35,000 –
–6   Cirrus
30,000 –
–5
25,000 –
Cirrostratus
–4
20,000 –
–3
15,000 –
–2
10,000 –
–1
5,000 –

Although the warm front has arrived high in the sky, it still has not arrived at ground level. As the wedge of the advancing warm air mass drops lower, the wispy cirrus clouds are thickening and becoming layered cirrostratus clouds. As the front approaches, the air pressure is dropping.

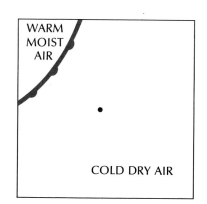

WARM
MOIST
AIR

COLD DRY AIR

/23

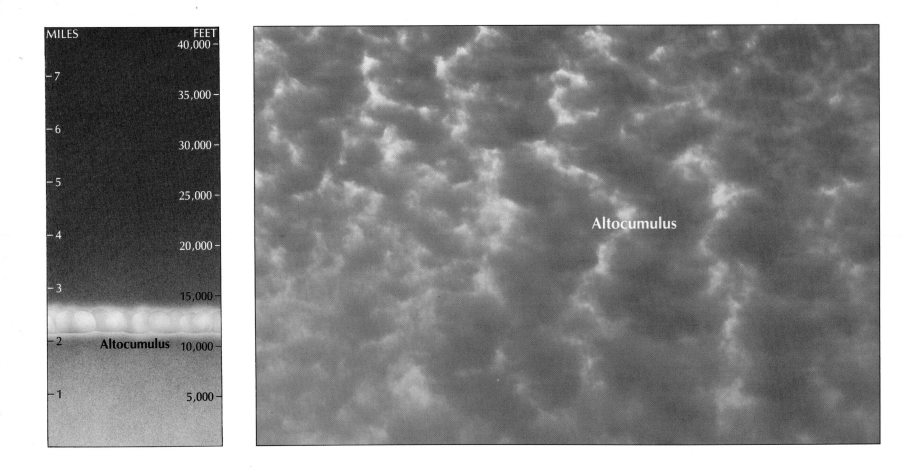

Altocumulus

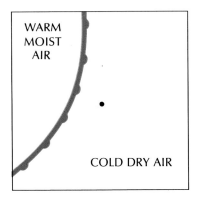

WARM
MOIST
AIR

COLD DRY AIR

The wedge of warm air continues to push over the cold air mass. The warm air mass slides up and over the cold air mass, cooling the warm, moist air and making more clouds. The high layer of cirrostratus clouds is followed by a lower layer of altocumulus clouds. The sky is becoming overcast.

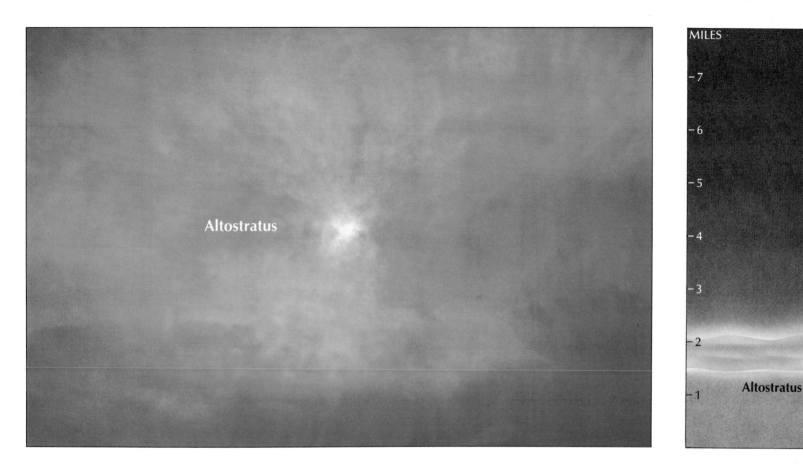

Altostratus

Altostratus clouds now appear at an even lower level. The sun can still be seen through the thin cloud layer. Because the air is winter-cold, ice crystals in the shapes of snowflakes are forming and the clouds are darkening. It's not snowing at ground level yet, but snow could be falling from the altostratus clouds and not reaching the ground. As it falls, the snow changes back into water vapor, which can then turn into more clouds.

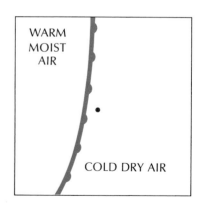

WARM
MOIST
AIR

COLD DRY AIR

Nimbostratus

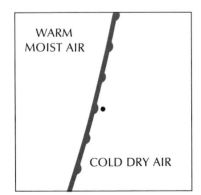

The warm front has arrived at your viewing place, and the clouds are thickening into a solid nimbostratus cloud layer. Above that, the unseen layer of altostratus clouds still remains. The sky is a solid sheet of gray. Ice crystals are developing in the nimbostratus cloud. When the crystals get large enough and heavy enough, they fall as snowflakes—it's snowing! Because nimbostratus snow clouds cover large areas, and because warm-front storms are slow-moving storms, it will snow for a long time. It will keep snowing until the clouds no longer have any moisture left or until the clouds move on to another place.

Stratus

MILES   FEET
40,000 –
– 7
35,000 –
– 6
30,000 –
– 5
25,000 –
– 4
20,000 –
– 3
15,000 –
– 2
10,000 –
– 1
5,000 –
Stratus

Eventually, the skies lighten and it stops snowing. The low stratus clouds are the last type in the warm-front sequence of clouds. With only a thin layer of stratus clouds remaining, the overcast sky is brightening. There are only snow flurries now. The warm air mass has arrived at ground level, and the winter day begins to feel warmer.

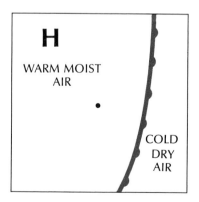

H

WARM MOIST AIR

COLD DRY AIR

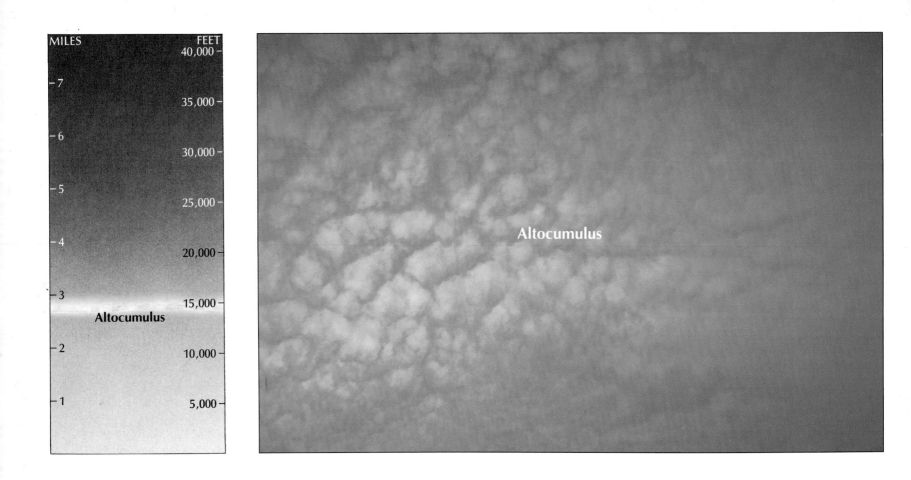

Altocumulus

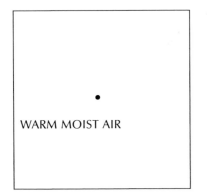

WARM MOIST AIR

Spring is here. Although the weak high of a warm, wet air mass is present and no fronts are approaching, the sky is not cloud-free. Middle-altitude altocumulus clouds have formed from some moisture present in the wet air mass. Though altocumulus clouds can mean snow or rain is on the way, it isn't always so. There are too many things interacting to affect the weather that could change this—such as highs moving in, weak warm fronts passing by, a stationary front causing no change, or one front overtaking another.

Altocumulus

Cirrostratus

MILES   FEET
                              40,000 —
— 7
                              35,000 —
— 6
                              30,000 —
— 5
              Cirrostratus
                              25,000 —
— 4
                              20,000 —
         Altocumulus
— 3
                              15,000 —
— 2
                              10,000 —
— 1
                               5,000 —

Often, there are many things going on at the same time in the sky, but at different heights. Air currents and very weak weather fronts that don't justify a line on the weather map still influence the local weather. Here, at the middle level of the sky, the waves of altocumulus clouds are breaking up. As these clouds of water droplets evaporate back into the atmosphere and that part of the sky clears, a thin layer of upper-level, ice-crystal, cirrostratus clouds is revealed.

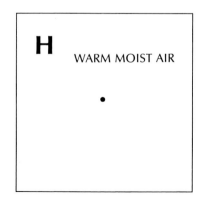

H WARM MOIST AIR

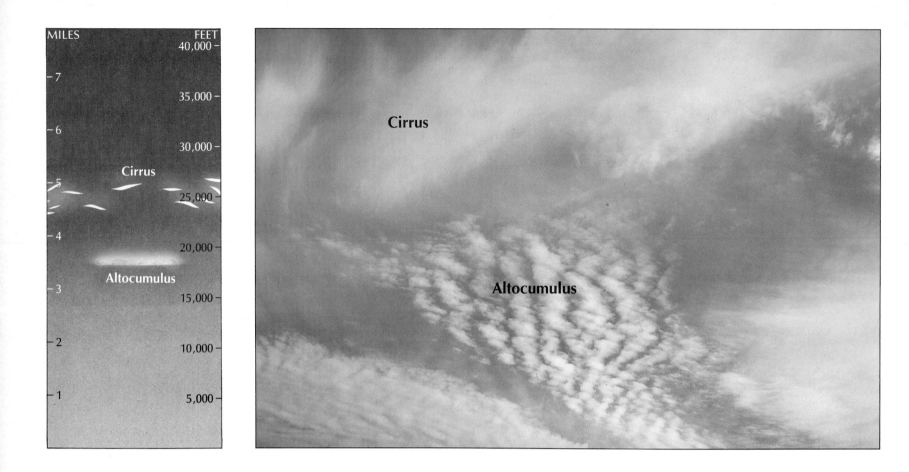

MILES | FEET
40,000 —
— 7
35,000 —
— 6
30,000 —
Cirrus
— 5
25,000 —
— 4
20,000 —
Altocumulus
— 3
15,000 —
— 2
10,000 —
— 1
5,000 —

Cirrus

Altocumulus

WARM MOIST AIR

· H

The last of the altocumulus clouds will soon be completely gone. The layer of cirrostratus clouds is becoming thinner, leaving only cirrus clouds to swirl about high in the sky. With the warmer season of spring, the top of the weather zone rises, and the cirrus clouds occur slightly higher than they do in the cooler seasons. In the summer, they will be even higher.

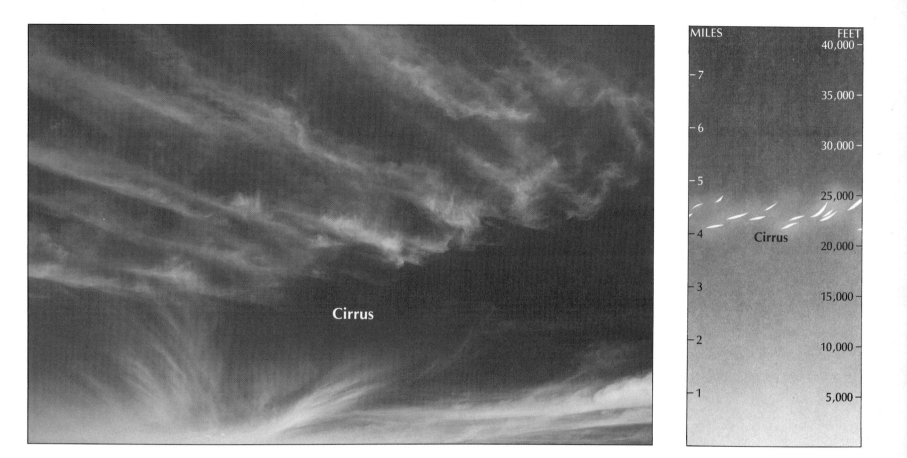

Cirrus

WARM MOIST AIR

• **H**

Because it's always freezing-cold at such a height—spring, summer, fall, and winter—upper-level clouds such as the cirrus clouds are made up of ice crystals. Sunlight reflects off the cirrus's ice crystals. That's why these clouds are always white, not gray.

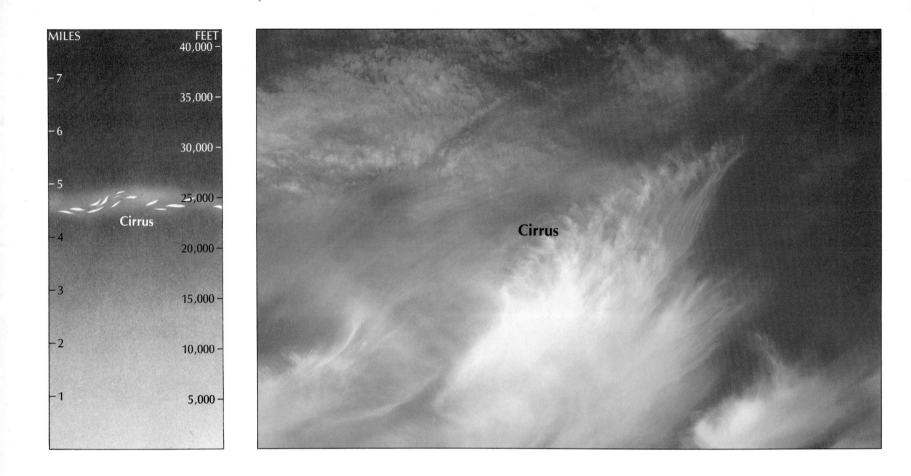

MILES | FEET

- 7
- 6
- 5
- 4
- 3
- 2
- 1

40,000 –
35,000 –
30,000 –
25,000 –
20,000 –
15,000 –
10,000 –
5,000 –

Cirrus

Cirrus

WARM MOIST AIR

. H

At the height of cirrus clouds, water vapor turns directly from a gas into solid ice crystals, with no liquid middle stage. The cirrus clouds' ice crystals can be seen as streaks of white blowing about and falling in the sky. But these falling ice crystals won't reach the ground. While still high above the ground, they change back from solid ice crystals into water vapor, and the crystals disappear.

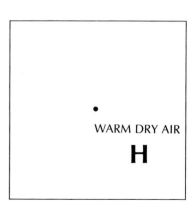

It's a clear day. The bright blue sky means the air is dry. It means the weather should stay clear—probably until a front arrives. No matter what the shade of blue, the blue sky is seen only during daylight hours because it's the sun's light that makes the sky blue. But stars are always above us in space, day or night. The blue light bouncing around the sky acts like a veil and keeps starlight from shining through to the earth's surface. The only star bright enough to penetrate the veil, and the same star that makes the sky blue, is our closest star—the sun.

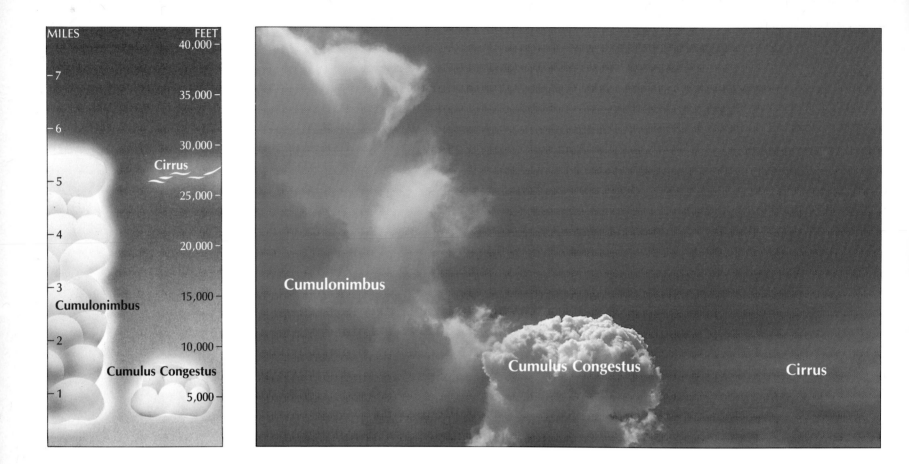

MILES | FEET

40,000 —

— 7

35,000 —

— 6

30,000 —

Cirrus

— 5

25,000 —

— 4

20,000 —

— 3

15,000 —

Cumulonimbus

— 2

10,000 —

Cumulus Congestus

— 1

5,000 —

Cumulonimbus

Cumulus Congestus

Cirrus

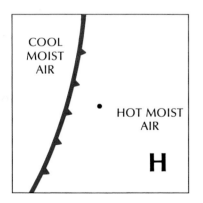

COOL
MOIST
AIR

HOT MOIST
AIR

H

Once again, the warmer weather of summer is arriving. At ground level, a fast-moving cold front is approaching. The high-altitude clouds, such as cirrus clouds, always appear white, but not middle- and low-altitude clouds. Low-altitude clouds, such as these cumulus congestus clouds, appear gray on the shadow side. Also, as storm clouds form, they become darker and darker overall. When the water droplets inside the clouds get larger and become heavy enough to form rain, instead of reflecting sunlight the now-dense clouds absorb it, and appear dark gray.

Cumulonimbus

Cumulonimbus

Cumulus Congestus

MILES   FEET

40,000 —

7

35,000 —

6

30,000 —

5

25,000 —

4

20,000 —

3

15,000 —

2

10,000 —

1

5,000 —

Cumulus Congestus

Inside the vertical space of the tall cumulonimbus clouds, the raindrops get larger and larger. Over and over again, they fall, get blown back by the updrafts of the cumulonimbus clouds, and become even larger. In the flat nimbostratus clouds of a warm front, there isn't as much vertical space, nor are there the strong updrafts. So raindrops formed during a cold-front storm are usually larger than raindrops formed during a warm-front storm.

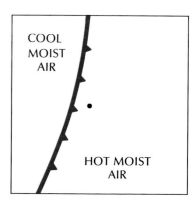

COOL
MOIST
AIR

HOT MOIST
AIR

Cumulus Congestus

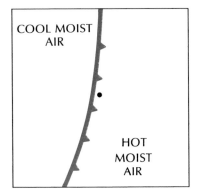

From the same storm, more cumulus congestus clouds, full of moisture, are passing by while billowing upward. They are developing into more cumulonimbus clouds, but these new clouds might not be just making rain. They might be making hail. Cumulonimbus clouds reaching the cold heights of the upper air layer can produce ice pellets of hail. Ironically, hail is seldom seen in the winter. It hails most often in the summer because cumulonimbus clouds occur most often during the warmer parts of the year. These clouds occur when it's warm because warm air can hold more moisture than cold air. Also, the vertical temperature contrast between ground level and the upper atmosphere is greatest during spring and summer. So cumulonimbus clouds are more vigorous then.

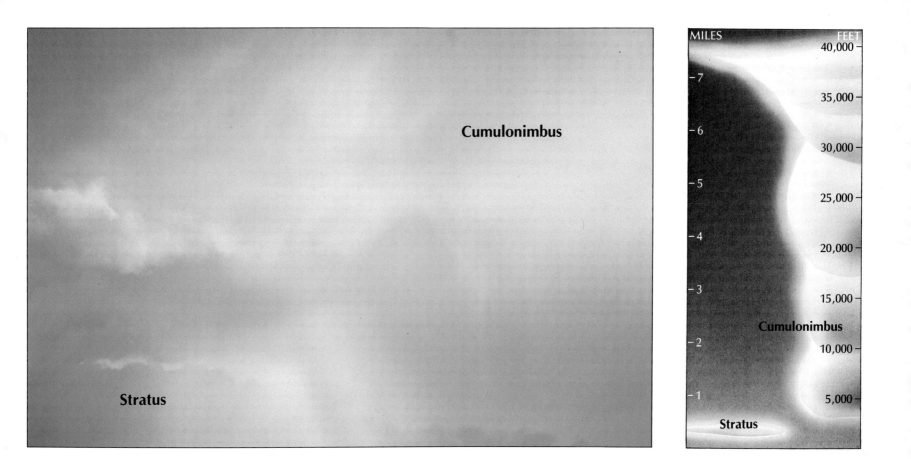

Cumulonimbus

Stratus

Cumulonimbus

Stratus

Cumulonimbus clouds are often the clouds that produce a beautiful sight in the weather sky—a rainbow. Two things are needed to make a rainbow: sunlight and water droplets. Because cold-front storms pass by quickly, the sun often shines while it's still raining, making a rainbow. In a single rainbow, like the one seen here, the outside color of the curve is always red. The arc of red color is made up of many raindrops bending and reflecting the red part of sunlight to where you view it. At the same time, other raindrops bend and reflect the rest of the colors of sunlight to display orange, yellow, green, blue, indigo, and, finally, violet at the inside of the rainbow's curve. The colors of a single rainbow always occur in this order.

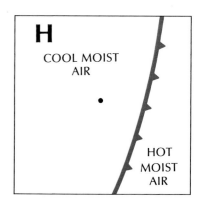

/37

Colorful and dramatic, a rainbow often foretells a clearing weather sky.

GLOSSARY

Air mass   A large body of air that floats across the earth's surface. It has layers of about the same temperature and moisture throughout.

Air pressure (atmospheric)   The force of the weight of air. Pressure is the weight of air overhead, measured as an imaginary column of air from the ground to the top of the atmosphere.

Atmosphere   The layer of gases that covers the earth, held there by gravity. In this book, the term refers to the lowest and densest layer of gases, from ground level to between six miles high at the poles and twelve miles high at the equator, specifically called the troposphere, or, more commonly, the weather zone. By volume, the weather zone is composed of nitrogen (78 percent), oxygen (21 percent), argon (1 percent), and other minor quantities of gases.

Cloud   A visible mist of water droplets or ice crystals floating in the weather zone.

Cold front   The leading edge of a cold air mass.

Front   The low-pressure area, forming a line, where two air masses contact each other, which often indicates a change in the weather. Usually there are contrasts in temperature and moisture across a front. Weather forecasters sometimes refer to a front as a trough.

High   An area of high air pressure located at the center of an air mass, usually indicating fair weather.

Low   An area of low air pressure, called a frontal low when it occurs along a front, usually indicating a change in weather.

Stationary front   A front that is stalled, with neither air mass advancing it.

Temperate climate   The earth's moderate climate that exists between the extremes of the hot equator and the cold North and South Poles.

Warm front   The leading edge of a warm air mass.

Weather   The state of the atmosphere at a certain place and time described by atmospheric phenomena such as the presence or absence of sunshine, clouds, rain, or snow.

INDEX

Page numbers in italics refer to illustrations and photographs.